I0010783

# KNOWING STRING MANIPULATION THROUGH C LANGUAGE

## (VOLUME #2-C-Series)

Copyright © 2018 By:

All rights reserved

**ISBN-13:**
**978-1722767921**

**ISBN-10:**
**1722767928**

# Dedication

**This book is created by Ch. Mamta Singha who is a student of BCA, residing in Silchar Assam (India). She is involved in many Java Projects and C Projects. This is dedicted to her:**

Mother: - Romabati Singha

Father: - Bhajahari Singha

Sister: - Romita Singha

**This book is created by Debajyoti Bhattacharjee who is a teacher , residing in Silchar Assam (India). He is involved in many Java Projects and C Projects. This is dedicted to his:**

Mother: -Manjushree Bhattacharjee

Father:- Lt. Niketan  Bhattacharjee

# CONTENTS OF TABLE

# Acknowledgement

We would like to express my special thanks of gratitude to our closest persons. We also thanks to our parents for their cordial supports. We Debajyoti Bhattacharjee and Mamta Singha begin to develop many books related to such fields and other programming books related to programs only.

# Chapter

# <u>About String</u>

## String :

String refers to the group of words which can be of meaningful or without meaning. String basically used to represent text and characters in programming language. It always carry multiple characters to named as string.  In other words strings are array but of character datatype.  An array of character is called string.  Strings are one dimensional array of character  which are terminated by null character represented by '\0'.

| ASCII |
|---|
| A-Z    =  65-90 |
| a- z   =  97-122 |
| 0-9    =  48-57 |

Ex : Physical representation of

**string of size 6 which conations string "Hello" in computer memory.**

| Address in computer memory |
|---|

| 600 | 601 | 602 | 603 | 604 | 605 |
|---|---|---|---|---|---|
| H | e | l | l | o | \0 |
| A[0] | A[1] | A[2] | A[3] | A[4] | A[5] |

Name of array

# Chapter

# Function of Strings

**There are basically four functions in String**

**1. Strlen()**

**2. Strcpy()**

**3. Strcat()**

**4. Strcmp()**

**strlen() :** This function is used to find the length of a String.

For ex :-

**Char str[5] = {"Hello"};**

**int l ;**

**l = Strlen(str);**

**strcpy() :** This function is used to copy String from one string variable to another string variable.

For ex :-

**Char str[5] = {"Hello"} , str2[6] = {"World"} ;**

**//Strcpy(destination , source);**

**Strcpy(str , str2);**

**strcat() :** This function is used to concat two string or to join two strings variable .

For ex :-

**Char str[5] = {"Hello"} , str2[6] = {"World"} ;**

**//Strcat(destination , source);**

**Strcpy(str , str2);**

**strcmp() :** This function is used to compare two string or to join two string variable.

For ex :-

**Char str[5] = {"Hello"} , str2[6] = {"World"} ;**

**//if (Strcmp (str , str2)==0)**

**Then both string variable are same**

**//if (Strcmp (str,str2)>0)**

**Then str is greater**

**//if (Strcmp (str,str2)<0)**

**Then str2 is greater**

# Chapter

## Programs using Functions

**1. Write a program to read and display string without any space.**

#include<stdio.h>

#include<conio.h>

#include<string.h>

void main()

{

char str [30];

clrcsr ();

printf ("\n Enter String :  ");

```
scanf ("%s",str);

printf ("\n You typed = %s ",str);

getch();

}
```

## 2. Write a program to read and display string with space.

```
#include<stdio.h>

#include<conio.h>

#include<string.h>

void main()

{

char str [30];
```

```
clrcsr ();

printf  ("\n Enter String :   ");

gets(str);

printf ("\n You typed = %s ",str);

getch();

}
```

## 3. Write a program to find the length of the String.

```
#include<stdio.h>

#include<conio.h>

#include<string.h>

void main()
```

```c
{
char str [30] , l;
clrcsr ();
printf ("\n Enter String :  ");
gets(str);
l  = Strlen(str);
printf("\n Length of String %s is %d ", str ,l  );
getch();
}
```

## 4. Write a program to read two string variables and concat or join them.

```c
#include<stdio.h>

#include<conio.h>

#include<string.h>

void main()

{

char str [30] , str1[30] ;

clrcsr ();

printf  ("\n Enter 1st  String :  ");

scanf ("%s",str);

printf ("\n Enter 2nd String :  ");

scanf("%d",str1);

strcat( str , str1);
```

Printf("\n Result after concatenation : %s ",str);

getch();

}


## 5. Write a program to copy a word from one string variable to another variable.

```
#include<stdio.h>

#include<conio.h>

#include<string.h>

void main()

{

char str [30] , str1[30] ;
```

```
clrcsr ();

printf  ("\n Enter 1st String :  ");

scanf ("%s",str);

printf("\n Enter 2nd String :  ");

scanf("%d",str1);

strcpy( str , str1);

Printf("\n Result after copying : %s ",str);

getch();

}
```

## 6. Write a program to check which string variable is greater.

```
#include<stdio.h>
```

```c
#include<conio.h>

#include<string.h>

void main()

{

char str [30] , str1[30] ;

clrcsr();

printf ("\n Enter 1st  String :  ");

scanf ("%s",str);

printf("\n Enter 2nd String :  ");

scanf("%d",str1);

if(strcmp (str , str1)>0)

{

printf("\n %s is greater ",str);
```

```
    }

    else

    {

    printf("\n %s is greater ",str1);

    }

    getch();

    }
```

## 7. Write a program to count the number of alphabet 'a' in a sentence .

```
#include<stdio.h>

#include<conio.h>

#include<string.h>
```

```c
void main()

{

char str [30] ;

int count=0 , l , i  ;

clrcsr ();

printf  ("\n Write a sentence :   ");

scanf ("%s",str);

l = strlen(str);

for(i=0  ; i<l ; i++)

{

If( str[i] == 'a')

  {

count++ ;
```

```c
    }

}

printf("\n Number of 'a' character in a sentence is  : %d ",count);

getch();

}
```

## 8. Write a program to count the number of vowels in a sentence.

```c
#include<stdio.h>

#include<conio.h>

#include<string.h>

void main()
```

```c
{

char str [30] ;

int count=0 , l , i  ;

clrcsr ();

printf  ("\n Write a sentence :  ");

scanf ("%s",str);

l = strlen(str);

for(i=0  ; i<l ; i++)

{

If( str[i] == 'a' || str[i] == 'e' str[i] == 'i' ||

str[i] == 'o' || str[i] == 'u')

   {

count++ ;
```

```
    }

}

printf("\n  Number  of  vowels  in  a
sentence is  : %d ",count);

getch();

}
```

**9. Write a program to count the number of  consonant   in a sentence .**

```
#include<stdio.h>

#include<conio.h>

#include<string.h>

void main()
```

```
{

char str [30] ;

int count=0 , l , i  ;

clrcsr ();

printf  ("\n Write a sentence :  ");

scanf ("%s",str);

l = strlen(str);

for(i=0  ; i<l ; i++)

{

If( str[i]   != 'a' || str[i]   != 'e' str[i]   != 'i'
|| str[i]  !='o' || str[i]  != 'u')

   {

count++ ;
```

```
    }

}

printf("\n Number of consonant in a
sentence is  : %d ",count);

getch();

}
```

## 10. Write a program to reverse a string.

```
#include<stdio.h>

#include<conio.h>

#include<string.h>

void main()

{
```

```
char str [30];

clrcsr ();

printf  ("\n Enter String :  ");

scanf ("%s",str);

strrev(str);

printf ("\n Reverse  string = %s ",str);

getch();

}
```

## 11. Write a program to change the string in both upper and lower case.

```
#include<stdio.h>

#include<conio.h>
```

```c
#include<string.h>
void main()
{
char str [30] , str1[30];
clrcsr();
printf ("\n String in lower case  :  ");
gets(str);
printf ("\n String in upper case  :  ");
gets(str1);
strupr(str);
strlwr(str1);
printf("\n Lower to upper case %s",str);
printf("\n Upper to lower case %s",str1);
```

```
getch() ;

}
```

## 12. Write a program to compare two string variables without case comparing.

```
#include<stdio.h>

#include<conio.h>

#include<string.h>

void main()

{

char str [30] ,  str1[30];

clrcsr();

printf  ("\n Enter 1st word  :  ");
```

```
gets(str);

printf ("\n Enter 2nd word :  ");

gets(str1);

if( strcmpi (str , str1)==0)

{

printf("\n Same ");

}

Else

{

printf("\n Not Same ");

}

getch();

}
```

# Chapter

## Logical Programs

**1. Write a program to print those character which lie on a even position**

#include<stdio.h>

#include<conio.h>

#include<string.h>

void main()

{

char str [30]

int  l , i , j;

```
printf  ("\n Enter any sentence  :  ");

gets(str);

l = strlen(str);

{

J=1+l;

If ( j % 2==0)

{

 printf  ("\n Character lies in even position %c ",str[i]);

}

getch();

}
```

## 2. Write a program to find specials, consonants, vowels, spaces and digits using switch.

```
#include<stdio.h>

#include<conio.h>

#include<string.h>

void main()

{

char str [30] ;

clrcsr();

int  l , i , count=0 ,v=0 ,c=0 , d=0, s=0, b=0;

printf ("\n Enter any sentence  :  ");

gets(str);
```

```
l=strlen(str);

for(i=0 ;i <l ; i++)

{

switch(str)

{
    case 'a' :

    case 'A' :

    case 'e' :

    case 'E' :

    case 'i' :

    case 'I' :

    case 'o' :

    case 'O' :
```

```
        case 'u' :

        case 'U' : v++;

break ;

        case '?' :

        case '\' :

        case '/' :

        case ',' :

        case '.' :

        case '%' :

        case ';' : s++;

break ;

        case '0' :

        case '1' :
```

```
case '2' :
case '3' :
case '4' :
case '5' :
case '6' :
case '7' :
case '8' :
case '9' : d++;
break;
case ' ' : b++;
default : c++;
}
}
```

```c
printf("\n Number of Vowels in a sentence : %d ",v);

printf("\n Number of Digits in a sentence : %d ",d);

printf("\n Number of Blank space in a sentence : %d ",b);

printf("\n Number of Special character in a sentence : %d ",s);

printf("\n Number of Other character in a sentence : %d ",c);

getch() ;

}
```

## 3. Write a program to arrange the name list in ascending order.

```
#include<stdio.h>

#include<conio.h>

#include<string.h>

void main()

{

char  name [30][30] ,temp[30];

int i ,n , j;

clrcsr ();

printf  ("\n Number of names :  ");

scanf ("%d ",&n);

for(i=0 ; i<n ; i++)
```

```c
{
printf ("\n Name[%d]  :  " ,(i+1));
scanf("%s ",name[i] );
}
for(i=0  ; i<n ; i++)
{
  for(j=1+I ; j<n-1 ; j++)
  {
   If( strcmp  (name[i], name[j])>0)
   {
strcpy(temp , name[i]);
strcpy(name[i] , name[j]);
strcpy(name[j] , temp);
```

```
    }

  }

}

for(i=0 ; i<n ; i++)

{

printf("\n %s ",name[i]);

}

getch();

}
```

**4. Write a program to delete those characters which are selected by the user from a sentence.**

```c
#include<stdio.h>

#include<conio.h>

#include<string.h>

void main()

{

char str [100], ch;

int  i, l;

clrcsr ();

printf  ("\n Enter Sentence :  ");

gets(str);

l=strlen(str);

printf("\n Enter the character you want
to delete :  ");
```

```
scanf("%c", &ch);

for( i=0 ; i<l ; i++)

{

If(str[i] == ch)

 {

str[i] = ' ';

 }

}

printf("\n  Result  after  deleting  the
character \n");

{

 If(str[i]  != ' ')

  {
```

```
printf("%c ",str[i]);

 }

}

getch();

}
```

**5. Write a program to check whether a given character is present in a string, find the frequency and position of the occurrence.**

```
#include<stdio.h>

#include<conio.h>

#include<string.h>
```

```c
void main()

{

char str[50], c;

int  i, l;

clrcsr();

printf("\n Type any string : ");

gets(str);

printf("\n Select any character form your string :  ");

scanf("%c ",&c);

l=strlen(str);

for(i=0 ; i<l ; i++)

{
```

```
If(str[i] == c)

{

printf("\n Yes %c character is present in %s in %d location " , str[i] , str , (i+1));

}

getch();

}
```

# Chapter

## Programs without using Functions

**1. Write a program to find the length of the String without using library function.**

```
#include<stdio.h>

#include<conio.h>

void main()

{

char  str [30] ;

int  i=0 , l=0 ;
```

```c
clrcsr ();

printf  ("\n Enter String :  ");

gets(str);

while( str[i] != '\0' )

{

  l++;

  i++;

}

printf("\n Length of String %s is %d ", str ,l  );

getch();

}
```

## 2. Write a program to copy a word from one string variable to another variable without using library function.

```c
#include<stdio.h>

#include<conio.h>

#include<string.h>

void main()

{

char  str [30] , str1[30] ;

int i=0, k=0;

clrcsr ();

printf  ("\n Enter 1st String :  ");

gets(str);
```

```
for(i=0 ; i<strlen(a) ; i++)

{

str1[k] = str[i] ;

k++;

}

b[k] = '\0';

printf("\n   Result   after   copying   :   %s ",str1);

getch();

}
```

**3. Write a program to read two string variables and concat or join them without using library function.**

```c
#include<stdio.h>

#include<conio.h>

#include<string.h>

void main()

{

char str [30] , str1[30] ;

int i=0 ,l1 ,l2 ,k;

clrcsr ();

printf ("\n Enter 1st  String :  ");

scanf ("%s",str);

printf ("\n Enter 2nd String :  ");

scanf("%d",str1);

l1 = strlen(str);
```

```c
a[k]= ' ' ;

k = k+1;

for(i=0 ; i<strlen(str1) ; i++)

{

str[k] = str1[i];

k++;

}

str[k] = '\0';

Printf("\n  Result  after  concatenation  :  %s ",str);

getch();

}
```

## 4. Write a program to reverse a string without using library function.

```c
#include<stdio.h>

#include<conio.h>

#include<string.h>

void main()

{

char a[30] , b[40];

int  i=0 , k=0;

clrcsr ();

printf  ("\n Enter String :  ");

scanf ("%s", &a);
```

```c
for(i= strlen(a)-1 ; i>=0 ; i--)

{

 b[k] = a[i];

k++;

}

b[k] = '\0' ;

printf ("\n Reverse  string = %s ",b);

getch();

}
```

**5. Write a program to compare two string variables without using function.**

```c
#include<stdio.h>
```

```c
#include<conio.h>

#include<string.h>

void main()

{

char a[30] ,  b[30];

int i=0 ,d1,d2,flag=0, l1, l2,j=0;

clrcsr();

printf  ("\n Enter 1st word  :  ");

scanf("%s ",a);

printf  ("\n Enter 2nd word :  ");

scanf("%s ",b);

l1 = strlen (a);

l2 = strlen (b);
```

```c
for(i=0 , j=0 ; i<l1 && l<l2 ;  i++, j++)

{

d1 = a[i];

d2 = b[j];

if(d1 == d2)

{

flag = 0;

}

else

{

flag=1;

break;

}
```

```
}

if( flag==0)

printf("\n Strings are equal ");

else

printf("\n Strings are not equal ");

getch();

}
```

# Chapter

# Project Work

1. **Write a program to demonstrate the operations of String in C program.**

```
#include <stdio.h>
#include <dos.h>
#include <conio.h>
#define   ESC 0x1b
#define   BSPACE 0x08
```

```cpp
const unsigned long far * const dosTime =
    (const unsigned long far * const)MK_FP( 0x40, 0x6C );

class Timer
{

public:

    Timer();
    void start();
    void stop();
    void reset();
    int status();
    double time();
```

```cpp
        static double resolution();
private:

        static unsigned adjust;
        static unsigned calibrate();
        int running;
        struct TIME
            {
            unsigned long dosCount;
            unsigned timerCount;
            };
        TIME startTime;
        double time_;
};


inline double Timer::time()
```

```
    {
        return time_/1.E6;
    }


    inline double Timer::resolution()
    {
        return 839/1.E9;
    }


    unsigned        Timer::adjust        =
    calibrate();

    Timer::Timer()        :        time_(0),
    running(0)
    {
    }
```

```
void Timer::start()
{
    if( !running )
        {
            outportb( 0x43, 0x34 );
            asm jmp __1;
    __1:
            outportb( 0x40, 0 );
            asm jmp __2;
    __2:
            outportb( 0x40, 0 );
            startTime.dosCount        =
*dosTime;
            startTime.timerCount = 0;
            running = 1;
```

```cpp
        }
    }

    void Timer::stop()
    {
        outportb( 0x43, 0 );
        unsigned  char  temp  =  inportb( 0x40 );

        TIME stopTime;
        stopTime.timerCount  =  (inportb( 0x40 ) << 8) + temp;
        stopTime.dosCount = *dosTime;

        TIME elapsedTime;
```

```c
    elapsedTime.dosCount       =
stopTime.dosCount              -
startTime.dosCount;
    elapsedTime.timerCount   =    -(
stopTime.timerCount - adjust );

    const    double    fudge    =
83810.0/100000.0;
    time_                    +=
((elapsedTime.dosCount << 16) +
elapsedTime.timerCount)*fudge;

    running = 0;

}
```

```
void Timer::reset()
{
    time_ = 0;
    if( running )
        start();
}

unsigned Timer::calibrate()
{
    adjust = 0;
    unsigned long sum = 0;
    Timer w;
    for( int i = 0; i < 100; i++ )
        {
        w.start();
        w.stop();
```

```
            sum += w.time();
            w.reset();
            }
        return (unsigned)((sum+5)/100);
    }


void main()
{
 clrscr();
 Timer t;
 char text[1000];
 int  i  =  0,  space_count  =  0,
letter_count = 0;
 float duration;
 printf("
```

# MDTECHNO PROGRAM TO CHECK TYPING SPEED

```
");
printf("Hit any key to start timer...

");
if(getch())
  {
    printf("Your time has started. Start typing. Hit Esc when done.

");
    t.start();
  }
while(1)
{
```

```c
    text[i] = getche();
  letter_count++;
  if(text[i] == ' ')
    space_count++;
  if(text[i] == '
')
    printf("
");
  if(text[i] == BSPACE)
    printf(" ");
  if(text[i] == ESC)
  {
    printf(" ");
    break;
  }
}
```

```
t.stop();
duration = t.time();
printf("

Your typing speed is :

");
printf("%6.2f      characters    per
minute
",60*letter_count/duration);
printf("%6.2f   words  per  minute
(Actual)
",60*space_count/duration);
```

```
    printf("%6.2f   words  per  minute
(Average)",60*letter_count/durati
on/5);

    getch();
}
```

**2. Write a program to demonstrate file handling using string only.**

```
#include<stdio.h>

#include<string.h>

#include<conio.h>

void main()
```

```c
{
char name [30];
char cls[10];
char tot[10],avg[10];
int i;
char grade[10];
FILE *fp;
fp=fopen("newstudent.txt","w");
clrscr();
for(i=0;i<5;i++)
{
printf("\n Enter Name  : ");
scanf("%s",name);
```

```c
fputs(name,fp);

fputs("\n",fp);

printf("\n Enter class : ");

scanf("%s",cls);

fputs(cls,fp);

fputs("\n",fp);

printf("\nEnter Percentage:");

scanf("%s",avg);

fputs(avg,fp);

fputs("\n",fp);

printf("\nEnter The Grade:");

scanf("%s",grade);

fputs(grade,fp);
```

```c
    fputs("\n--------------",fp);

}

fclose(fp);

getch();

}
```

# Chapter

# Self Exercise

1. C program to swap two Strings

2. C Program to Sort an array of names or strings

3. C Program to Check if a Given String is Palindrome

4. C Program for Return maximum occurring character in the input string

5. C Program for Remove all duplicates from the input string.

6. C Program for Print all the duplicates in the input string.

**7.** C Program for Remove characters from the first string which are present in the second string

**8.** C Program for A Program to check if strings are rotations of each other or not

**9.** C Program for Write a C program to print all permutations of a given string

**10.** C Program for Divide a string in N equal_parts

**11.** C Program for Given a string, find its first non-repeating character

**12.** C Program for Print list items containing all characters of a given word

**13.** C Program for Reverse words in a given string

**While solving above questions find any questions or doubts ask us on using below:**

Contact:

**9706302163**

**7636982826**

Email Id:

bdebajyoti@hotmail.com

singhamamta915@gmail.com

# CONCLUSION

This 2<sup>nd</sup> Volume of "C-Series" was published by Mr. Debajyoti Bhattacharjee and Mamta Singha. This also gets extended in future after publishing the 3<sup>rd</sup> Volume known as "Matrix Manipulations through C Language: Experiencing C Language Phase-#1".

Please Do Support us for such contributions.

www.ingramcontent.com/pod-product-compliance
Lightning Source LLC
Chambersburg PA
CBHW041430050326

40690CB00002B/495